For my father.

Puppies chew shoes, don't they?

A user's manual for people with puppies.

DEE BOGETTI

They were puppies once.

These are my Labs. Cody (left), whose face has turned almost entirely white with age, is 13 and still going strong. Murphy is nine. He keeps things light and loving and will forever be ... a puppy. Both of these wonderful dogs came to me at 8 weeks of age. The journey I've been on with them has been the best of my life. I wish you the same with your puppy.

In the picture at right, Cody plays "catch me if you can" with Murphy when they were young. He never caught her. She could run like the wind.

Nani, the third Lab in our house, came to live with us four years ago. She was five and had lost her home because of a divorce. She had gone there as a puppy and I'm sure, didn't understand why she had to leave. She is shy and sweet. She is also Murphy's littermate.

GREETINGS and welcome to my very doggy world. In my world, dogs live happily ever after in their forever homes. In my world, dogs play and work and are part of the family. In my world, dogs are not disposable.

In the larger world, too many dogs are misunderstood and are far too often thrown away for no reason other than lack of knowledge on their human's part. After being called in hundreds of times to help people with a "problem" puppy, it became clear that these families hadn't the faintest idea how to raise a puppy.

So, here's the thing. If you start a puppy right, you have a good chance at having a great adult dog. That's why I wrote *Puppies chew shoes, don't they?.* There are many resources out there to help you teach your puppy how to sit, down, stay, come and every other obedience skill on the planet. Instead of telling you HOW to train specific skills (with a few exceptions), I'm hoping to help you understand:

- Why your puppy pulls on leash and how to fix that;
- Why he pees in the house and how to avoid that;
- Why crate training is totally cool;
- How to create a polite puppy with exquisite house manners;
- And much more.

If you understand your puppy and learn to communicate with him, you have a better chance of being a successful puppy parent.

As we begin, remind yourself that your puppy's first year will be magical. Try to see the world through his eyes: the first leaf he watches fall to earth, his first encounter with a squirrel, the first time he splashes in a puddle. That first year is full of sparkle and shine and promise. Be part of it. And take lots of pictures. His time as a puppy will fly by.

Now ... let's talk puppy.

Dee

Contents

Most of the photos in this book are of puppies with whom I've worked as a trainer. My thanks to them and their people for making my life extraordinary for having known them. This book is dedicated to all of them. A special "paws up" to Kim & Lily (left) and Jacob & Shalom (above).

Relax. You can do this.

He's just a puppy.

You're bigger than him.

And you have thumbs!

Chapter 1
Warning: puppy on the loose!

YOUR PUPPY ARRIVED five minutes ago. You plunked the little darling in the middle of the floor for all to adore and ... he peed. You admire the fact that his plumbing works. He turns, snags your pant leg (it was the closest thing to him) and pulls. You screech, laugh, and disengage your brand new puppy from your clothing.

Fast forward a few weeks and Cute Adorable Puppy has used your entire house as a toilet, pooping and peeing wherever he chooses. He has destroyed two books, a shoe, the remote, your favorite Bog Seger CD, most of a pillow, three rolls of toilet paper, and is working on gnawing through the legs of your dining room table. Do you have a bad puppy? **No.** A stupid puppy? **Probably not.** A normal puppy? **Most likely, yes.**

So what's up with all this? To start with, your puppy:

- Came to this unfamiliar place – your home – without his mom or siblings and he's adjusting
- Has no idea what language you're speaking (think English-speaking American in Moscow, trying to understand Russian)
- Hasn't a clue what a collar and leash are, much less why he's forced to wear them
- Sleeps, plays, poops, pees, eats … and then does it all over again
- Is a baby, so cut him some slack

Whether you got your puppy from a breeder, a rescue or your neighbor, assume your puppy has never worn a collar or set foot in a crate, nor is he potty trained. You are starting with raw material.

TIME TO REWIND THE TAPE. Your new puppy will arrive in a week. What should a responsible pet parent do to prepare?

Puppy-proof your home

Get on your hands and knees to look at your house from a puppy's perspective. Even if you tether your puppy to you and crate train him, sometime in his youth he will escape your watchful eye and destroy something you are fond of – if he can reach it. Starting now, make sure anything important to you, or dangerous to him, *isn't* within his reach.

Since you have been warned, when your puppy rips apart a pair of $100 shoes, here's what you do: roll up a newspaper and smack yourself upside the head. It's YOUR fault, not his! Why? Because Puppy Rule #1 is: If it fits in his mouth and he can reach it, it will *go* in his mouth. And there are teeth in there. Sharp ones that can destroy an amazing array of your things. So the answer to the question "Puppies chew shoes, don't they?" is ... absolutely!

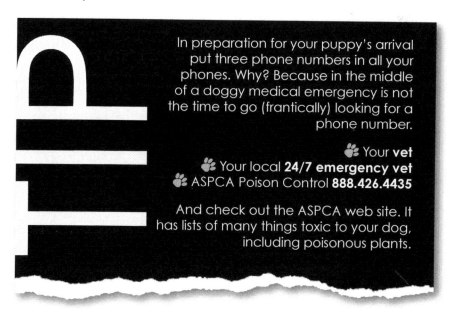

In preparation for your puppy's arrival put three phone numbers in all your phones. Why? Because in the middle of a doggy medical emergency is not the time to go (frantically) looking for a phone number.

🐾 Your **vet**
🐾 Your local **24/7 emergency vet**
🐾 ASPCA Poison Control **888.426.4435**

And check out the ASPCA web site. It has lists of many things toxic to your dog, including poisonous plants.

In addition to shoes, puppies will happily chew and sometimes ingest:

- Computer cables and electric cords
- Articles of clothing (underwear is a puppy favorite)
- Sporting equipment
- Children's toys
- Books, magazines, newspapers, DVDs, CDs, homework
- Fingers, arms, toes, legs
- Other family pets
- Pant legs and chair legs
- Remote controls
- Electronics: cell phones, tablets, e-readers, etc.
- Eye glasses
- Leashes and collars
- Contents of litter boxes ("dog candy")
- Food of any kind – dog, cat, bird, gerbil, fish, human
- Plants (beware, some houseplants are toxic to dogs)
- Anything at puppy nose level

What do you do to prevent total destruction of your worldly possessions? For starters, your puppy should have limited access to your home. Close doors to bedrooms, bathrooms, your home office and the kids' playroom. And put a baby gate at the top and bottom of stairs. If you have cats, put their food and litter box where your cats can reach them but your puppy can't.

All trash cans should be out of reach. Raiding them is self-rewarding for a puppy and once he has experienced those trash can delights, it can be a real challenge to get him to stop.

Outdoors. If you have a swimming pool, make sure your puppy cannot get into it when unsupervised. Introduce your puppy to your pool carefully, showing him how to get out, as well as how to get in. Those stairs are obvious to you but not to your puppy. Also, puppies have no depth perception, which is why one will occasionally try to walk on water.

This can result in a very surprised puppy when he is suddenly *under* water. That experience can create a puppy who is afraid of *all* water: pools, rivers, lakes, the ocean and ... baths. So ease him into the pool supporting his chest and belly. A floating long line (aka, floating check cord) attached to his collar will insure his safety as he starts to swim away from you that very first time. Be aware that not all dogs like the water – no matter how much *you* do. And unless you plan to train your dog for water rescue (that thing Newfoundlands do so well), it's okay if your dog doesn't want to swim. So, watch out for flailing puppy legs. That's a sign that your puppy may prefer dry land. If he gets frightened and tries desperately to find a way out of the pool, he will likely scratch anyone blocking his way. If this happens, get behind him and guide him to the nearest safe place for him to exit the pool.

Yards are full of things puppies like to investigate. Make sure anything toxic to dogs (fertilizer, pesticides, antifreeze) is out of reach. If your yard is fenced, make sure there are no spaces a puppy can squeeze through. Do you have a fence, deck or balcony with verticals far enough apart for your puppy to escape? Consider a Puppy Bumper ... a stuffed safety collar that attaches to your puppy's existing collar.

Daisy demonstrates a Puppy Bumper. They're great not only for puppies but for small breed dogs of all ages.
www.puppybumpers.net

Do you leave your rake and gardening tools out in your backyard? Based on my experience with one of my Lab puppies, put them away. Their handles make fabulous chew toys.

Be aware that if you *do* have a yard, your new puppy may dig holes, bed down in the flowers, chew the corners off of your deck steps, and bark at everything from butterflies to falling leaves. He may eat dirt and rocks and parts of trees. He is, after all, a puppy. And EVERYTHING is fascinating to him. Supervise him outdoors to make sure he doesn't get bored – which will inevitably lead to him getting into trouble.

Buy the basics before your puppy arrives

Wherever your puppy is coming from – breeder, rescue, foster family, a friend – ask what kind of food he's eating and buy a supply of that. You don't want to upset your puppy's tummy by changing his food right away. Keep your puppy's food in a sealed container well away from your puppy's prying nose. Puppies have been known to find a bag of dog food, rip into it, and gorge themselves ... followed by a swollen abdomen and often a great deal of vomiting and pooping.

Get **food and water bowls** and put then where you want your puppy to eat and drink, preferably on a tile floor that won't be harmed by a sloppy puppy. Water bowls can be a great source of fun for puppies who like to splash in them. And some will drag a light-weight bowl all around the house. So start with a heavy stainless steel or ceramic bowl or a no-tip bowl like the one shown here. Still no guarantees there won't be a mess but it will be a little less likely with the right bowls. Another issue for new puppy parents is the puppy who snarfs his food so fast he nearly (or

The Tricky Treat Ball is one of my favorite interactive toys. It has one hole to put your puppy's dry food into: one way in, one way out. Your puppy will learn to roll it and toss it in the air to get the food out. It will keep him entertained for a bit while you're starting dinner, checking e-mails, etc.

Dog puzzles are everywhere these days. The one at right is typical: you put treats in the recessed areas, cover them up with the "bone" puzzle pieces and put it on the floor for your dog to figure out how to get the treats. Warning: don't leave your puppy alone with these puzzles. The parts can be destroyed by puppy teeth and you don't want pieces of them in your puppy's belly.

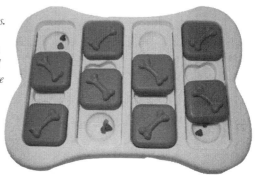

actually does) choke on it. This applies to almost all Labrador retrievers and lots of their relatives. There are entire lines of dog food bowls available to slow those snarfers down. Check out Kyjen slow feeders as an example of what's out there.

Or ... feed your puppy from an interactive toy like a Kong. This is not a new idea but it's a great one. Here's how it worked with a puppy who was at my house for a few days of "board and train" between the time he left his breeder and the time he went to his new home. In the photo at right, you see Astro's introduction to eating his dog food out of a Kong. I measured his food for the whole day every morning. He got a Kong full of dry food for breakfast, lunch and dinner, with the remainder used as training treats throughout the

day. I always had a pocket full of his food, in case he did something brilliant that I wanted to reward. Read more about this Aussie puppy at **browndogtales.blogspot.com**. Keyword: Astro 🐾

Please, please, please **crate train** your puppy. You'll never regret it. A dog's crate isn't his prison. Really it's not. Rather, it's his safe place. And I promise you, life will be far easier throughout your puppy's first year if you can plunk him in his crate any old time – and he's happy to be there.

It took no time at all for Astro, the Aussie puppy, to connect his food, the Kong, and his crate. He was tethered to me in the house (learning house manners – we'll address that later), which means we went together to the location of his Kong and his puppy food. While I loaded the Kong, he sat and watched. When I finished, I dropped his leash and he raced to his crate, getting there well before me. Waiting in happy anticipation and in full wag, he sat for me while I removed leash and collar and put his Kong in the crate. When I released him from his sit (I use the phrase "free dog" when I teach puppies to stay put until I tell them to do something else), in he went, settling in immediately with his Kong. I closed the crate door, latched it, and went about my business.

Think about mornings with your puppy. If that part of your day is hectic – getting kids ready for school or yourself ready for work – crating your puppy with his breakfast served in a Kong could simplify things.

A few words about choosing a crate ... I suggest that you get a wire crate sized to fit your dog as an adult. Get one with a movable divider that you can adjust as your puppy grows. My favorite has at least two doors – one in the front, one on the side. Two doors make it really easy to get your puppy in and out of his crate, even when you put it into a space sideways (like in the back of an SUV).

If you have a large home or one with multiple levels, consider getting two crates – one for your bedroom and one for your primary living area.

Puppies sometimes settle quicker and easier if you're in sight. Sometimes not. Think about when you're working in the kitchen. Your puppy can be in a crate nearby, keeping an eye on you – but not underfoot. What about when the kids get home from school, there's a lot going on in your main living area, and your puppy is cranky because he needs a nap? That's when you put him in the crate in your bedroom, turn off the light, maybe turn on a radio, close the door, and let him take his nap in peace and quiet. *You'll find more on crate training in Chapter 2.* 🐾

Get your puppy an inexpensive **leash** and **collar**. Why not get the designer version right off the bat? Because your puppy will chew on (and likely through) at least one leash and you'll have to replace it. And he'll outgrow his new collar almost immediately and you'll have to replace that. Go ahead and start a bin or cardboard box for discarded items that your puppy no longer needs. By the time he's a year old, you will likely have a nice donation for your local rescue.

A couple of **toys** like a tennis ball and a squeaky toy are perfect when you first bring your puppy home. Make sure someone is with him when he plays with anything that can be shredded or taken apart. Why? Because if your puppy swallows something he shouldn't, it may or may not pass through him and come out the other end. Puppies get blockages all the time from ingesting stuff they shouldn't. And you don't want your puppy in surgery before he's even potty trained.

Dogs laugh,

but they laugh with their tails.

~Max Eastman

Be prepared for the cost

Puppies are expensive little darlings. Typical costs associated with a puppy's first year include:

- Three sets of vaccinations
- Micro-chipping
- Spay or neuter
- Flea, tick and heartworm preventative
- Food
- Treats
- Brush or comb, nail clippers and shampoo (if you plan to do your own grooming) or the cost of professional grooming
- Crate(s)
- Food and water bowls
- Collar and leash (not a retractable)
- Toys
- Obedience classes and/or private training

- More collars (when he outgrows the original) and leashes (when he chews through the original)
- Back and/or front yard fencing to keep him safe
- Boarding or pet sitting when you travel

You might also want to consider health insurance for your puppy. The industry is growing so fast, there is no data I can give you that I can guarantee will still be accurate by the time this book is published. If you're interested, do an internet search for "health insurance for dogs" and comparison shop.

Choose the right veterinarian

You will spend quite a bit of time in your vet's office during your dog's life. Consider shopping around for the right vet before your puppy comes home. Look into an American Animal Hospital Association (AAHA) accredited vet practice or an integrative veterinarian (find one online through the Veterinary Institute of Integrative Medicine). Most important, look for a vet who is up on current veterinary medicine and loves dogs. A good vet's kindness goes a long way when your dog is getting shots or is sick or injured.

Schedule your puppy's first appointment for a few days after you bring him home. At that first wellness visit, ask questions about vaccinations, spaying (girl puppies) or neutering (boy puppies), flea and tick protection, heartworm preventatives, etc.

One last word about veterinarians and other dog professionals: don't be afraid to ask questions. And know that it's okay to fire a vet, a trainer, a groomer or anyone else whose methods you don't like. Take charge of your puppy's well-being from the beginning. 🐾

Get the family together ...

Take the time to sit down with all the members of your family, extended family, and friends and decide what the house rules will be for your puppy and the people who interact with him. Here's an example of the kind of thing to think about: either your puppy is allowed on the furniture or he isn't. You will *totally* confuse him if some members of the family allow him to join them on the sofa while others yell at him for doing the same thing. Get off to a really good start with your puppy and teach him he's only allowed on furniture when he's invited. Teach your puppy "up" and "off" early on and you'll have a grown-up dog who never gets on furniture uninvited. *Learn more about house manners in Chapter 5.* 🐾

Now it's time. Get ready, get set ... bring that puppy home!

Chapter 2
The basics

WHAT ARE THE MOST IMPORTANT THINGS to teach your puppy? Start with these:

- **Potty and crate training** are #1 and shouldn't take more than a week or two to accomplish.
- **House manners** will save your sanity.
- If you teach no other obedience skill, teach **sit** as your puppy's default behavior.
- Start teaching your puppy how to **walk on a leash** without pulling the very first time you put a leash on him.

Potty training

Potty training a puppy is the pretty much the same as teaching a puppy to do anything else (like sit or come). And as with *all* dog training, it requires a lot of:

Patience ❧ Persistence ❧ Consistency

Here are some tried and true techniques to help you successfully potty train your puppy.

Give it a name. Call it "go potty", "outside", "baseball", anything you like, but do it consistently.

Same place every time. Take your puppy outside to go potty *on leash* to the same place every time. You have a bathroom. He needs one, as well. One that is clearly defined. Why on leash? First, you need to see what's coming out of your puppy those first few weeks. Is he peeing too much? Urinary tract infections (UTIs) are common in puppies (especially females but males get them, too) and often go undiagnosed. If your puppy pees in his crate or in your house and you are being vigilant about taking him *out* to potty, take a urine sample to your vet for testing. Are his stools soft or does he have diarrhea? It is also fairly common for puppies to have parasites – some of which can cause diarrhea. If your puppy has diarrhea, collect a stool sample and take it to your vet for testing. The other reason you may want to take your puppy out to potty on leash is to teach him the specific place you want him to go ... unless you want piles of dog poop all over your yard.

Reward, reward, reward. Take treats outside with you. When puppy pees or poops in the right place, give him a food reward and use your happy voice with lots of "atta boys!". Wait until your puppy is finished peeing or pooping to reward him, as interrupting the process can result in a puppy who never gets to finish outside, so he does so inside. You should only have to use food rewards for a week or two. Most puppies get the idea pretty quickly. The general rule is that a puppy who has to pee will do so within a minute or two. Poop usually comes happens within five minutes.

Each week that your puppy grows older, his body parts grow bigger. A puppy who has to go out every four hours at eight weeks may be able to go six hours (and sometimes more) between potty breaks by the time he's ten weeks. The best gauge of this is to pay attention to the time you put your puppy to bed – in a crate in your bedroom – and what time he stirs. Generally, the only thing that wakes a young puppy up in the middle of the night is the urge to pee. If you hear toenails clicking in his crate, take him out. If you just here him move a bit, he's probably repositioning. You may be surprised how quickly your puppy can sleep through the night without a potty break.

Limited access. Until potty training is complete, limit your puppy's access to your home. Use baby gates to prevent your puppy from going up and down stairs. Close doors to rooms puppy should not be in.

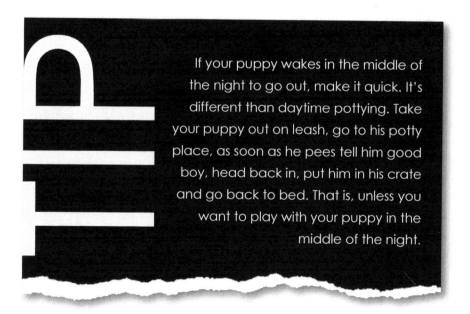

If your puppy wakes in the middle of the night to go out, make it quick. It's different than daytime pottying. Take your puppy out on leash, go to his potty place, as soon as he pees tell him good boy, head back in, put him in his crate and go back to bed. That is, unless you want to play with your puppy in the middle of the night.

Tethering. Try tethering your puppy to you. This will prevent potty accidents and property damage (furniture legs and the edges of rugs are popular with puppies). You can run your belt through the loop of a four-foot leash or use a hands-free leash that goes around your waist or over your shoulder and across your chest. *More on tethering in Chapter 5.*

Ignore unwanted behavior. Puppies get this if you do it consistently: reward wanted behavior, ignore unwanted behavior. This applies to everything, including potty training. Your puppy wants your attention and will get it any way that works. If you make a big deal out of your puppy going potty in the house, you are in a very strange way rewarding the behavior. Even if you yelled at him when he peed in the living room (a totally worthless training method, by the way), your puppy got your attention – which is what he wanted. Besides it wasn't his fault. Most puppy potty training accidents happen because the person in charge of the puppy wasn't paying attention. So pay attention, tether and crate your puppy appropriately, learn his pee schedule, and all will be well.

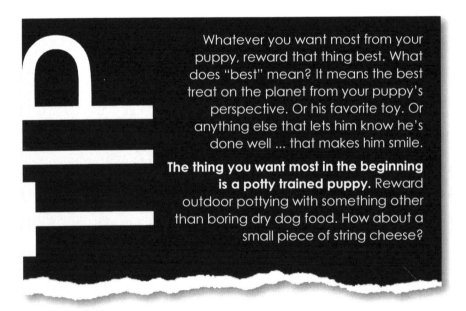

Whatever you want most from your puppy, reward that thing best. What does "best" mean? It means the best treat on the planet from your puppy's perspective. Or his favorite toy. Or anything else that lets him know he's done well ... that makes him smile.

The thing you want most in the beginning is a potty trained puppy. Reward outdoor pottying with something other than boring dry dog food. How about a small piece of string cheese?

Clear communication between you and your puppy will make potty training easier. If you teach your puppy to ring a bell attached to a door, he can tell you every time he needs to go out. Here are the steps:

- Take your puppy out the same door every single time you take him outside for a potty break. Within a couple of days, he will know that when that particular door opens, he gets to go outside – which most puppies love to do. Most likely he will start gravitating toward that door when he has to go potty.

- Get a bell. It doesn't have to be anything fancy, only something loud enough for you to hear throughout your house. And don't make it so big your puppy can't easily set it ringing with paw or nose.

- Hang the bell on the "go outside" door knob at puppy-nose-height. Or hang it on a hook on the wall or even from the ceiling. The only thing that matters is that your puppy can see the bell as he approaches the door and can ring it with paw or nose *without jumping*.

- When you get ready to take your puppy outside for a potty break, put on his leash, approach the door, and jingle the bell(s). Your puppy, being the curious sort, will most likely touch the bell with his nose. If he does (even if it doesn't ring), open the door and in your happiest voice, with a spring in your step, take puppy with you, telling him he is brilliant for ringing the bell.

- Repeat until your puppy rings the bell on his own.

Your puppy should be completely potty trained in a couple of weeks. If he's not, maybe it's time to find a trainer to come to your home and evaluate what's going on. 🐾

Crate training

Choosing a crate. The two most popular crates are wire and molded plastic. They come in sizes to accommodate most any dog and are available at pet stores and online. A dog's crate should be just big enough for him to stand up, turn around, and lay down. If you choose a wire crate, get one with dividers – based on your pup's estimated size as an adult (like the one we talked about in Chapter 1). This kind of crate allows you to block off one end of the crate while your pup is small. Otherwise, he may use one end of a too-large crate as a toilet and the other end as a bedroom. The best wire crates have at least two doors – end and side. Always remove puppy's leash and collar before crating to prevent choking.

Make it fun. Place the crate in an area of your house where the family spends a lot of time. Lure your puppy over to the crate with a treat or his favorite toy, talking to him in your happy voice.

- Sit quietly on the floor next to the crate for a few minutes while puppy is noodling in and out of it. Toss a toy in the crate. Make it the best puppy den ever.
- Getting comfortable in there, is he? Close the crate door for a minute or two at a time. Don't leave the room just yet.
- Next time, crate puppy, close the crate door and go to another room for a few minutes. Return quietly and let him out of the crate.

Always use a verbal cue: point to the crate and say the word(s) that will direct your pup to go in the crate. "Kennel up" is my personal favorite. Always ask puppy to "wait" before exiting his crate. This eliminates pushy-puppy syndrome and begins the process of teaching your puppy to wait before going out any door and before entering or exiting a vehicle. Polite puppy syndrome. We like that.

Repeat this process often. With each repetition, gradually increase the length of time you leave your puppy in the crate and the length of time you're out of sight. When your puppy can spend 30 minutes in the crate without becoming anxious or afraid, you can begin crating him for short periods when you leave the house. Very soon you will have a pup who loves his crate. Happy happy joy joy! Learn a bit more about crates at **puppieschewshoes.blogspot.com**. Keyword: crates

Now, what if – on the Monday after you get your puppy – – everyone has to go back to work or school. Your puppy can't be left loose in your house, so you have to crate him. All day? Not good. Instead, do you have a small bathroom you puppy-proof? That means removing toilet paper, bath mats, trash can, shower curtains, towels, soaps, shampoos, etc. Anything at all your puppy can put in his mouth or get into. Provide water and safe interactive toys. Put a baby gate on the door. Try this out prior to Monday morning to make sure it works for your puppy.

So, what comes after the basics: potty and crate training? Everything else. Let's move along to house manners, obedience training and the concept of teaching a puppy self-control.

Chapter 3
Let the training begin

HAVE YOU EVER KNOWN A DOG who was totally cool? One who seemed to always be happy, never pestered anyone for attention, and didn't bark incessantly? One who liked people and other dogs and even cats but didn't jump on or chase any of the above? Do you want that dog?

If you've had dogs all your life, you may have gotten lucky and had one who came to you as perfect as a dog can be. I had one. His name was Maxx. All of my other dogs have required a lot of training. So if you don't have a Maxx, let's talk.

Having observed a lot of people and their puppies, I know that after potty and crate training, teaching house manners is the most important thing we can do to create great dogs from goofy puppies.

Where to start? **Teach sit.**
That's my Murphy at right
when he was a wee lad. He's
nine years old now. He's had
a long working life: therapy
dog, spokes-dog for nonprofits,
demo dog, assistant trainer
(helping clients' dogs
overcome scary stuff), and
service dog. His training
began at eight weeks of age,
with sit.

As I've worked with puppies
over the years, I noticed that
many of them will trot up to
a person, sit and look up. If
the person doesn't respond
quickly, the puppy will do
something else. He will likely replace sitting with jumping. After all,
sitting politely got him nothing, right?

If you are lucky enough to have a puppy who sits automatically in front
of you, be prepared to respond. Keep some of his dry dog food or treats
in your pocket. If you don't have a pocket, get yourself a treat pouch to
use as you start training house manners. Here's where to start.

Each morning, measure out a day's worth of puppy food. Let's say you
feed two cups a day. Feed him three-quarters of a cup in the morning
and another three-quarters cup at night. Put the remaining half cup in
your pocket or a treat pouch. Use this food throughout the day to reward
your puppy when he does something good. That means, when your
puppy comes running up to you and instead of jumping, he sits, you're
prepared. *As it's happening*, reach in pocket or pouch and pull out a treat.

Teaching a puppy to do something when you tell him to (giving him a command) means the puppy has to learn words that go with actions.

This won't work if you have to move away from your puppy to get the treat. Since your puppy's sit won't last long, immediately say something like "good sit". Reach down with one hand to give him an "atta boy" pat while bringing your other hand, open palm with treat in it, under his chin. That open palm will likely prevent your puppy from nipping your fingers when taking the treat. The position of your hand (under his chin) will also discourage standing or jumping. As soon as he's eaten his treat, tell him he's a good boy one more time, say "free dog" (you've just started teaching a release word) and walk away. In those few seconds (it happens fast and you have to respond fast), you are teaching your puppy what sit means, that sit gets rewarded, and that you're paying attention. Adding the release word, you're also telling your puppy he's all done for now. Bravo.

Check out the best treat pouch ever at **puppieschewshoes.blogspot. com**. Keyword: treat pouch

Teaching a puppy to do something when you tell him to (giving him a command) means the puppy has to learn words that go with actions. For example, sit is the word that goes with the action of the puppy putting his butt on the floor or ground. Every time you see him sit, say something like "good sit". Soon he'll connect the word and the action and respond when you give him the command.

The next step is: When your puppy knows what sit means, give the command, wait for the sit to happen, then give the puppy something he wants. Let's say he sat beautifully, so now he gets to chew on his antler.

If the sit doesn't happen immediately, be patient. And don't nag. Sit-sit-sit-sit-sit-sit-sit (repeating the command over and over) is nagging. Instead, say your puppy's name. Use your happy voice. When he looks at you, say sit and take a small step toward him, getting a bit closer. Now, count out ten seconds (in your head, not out loud) like this: one good dog, two good dog, three good dog, etc. If during those ten seconds, your puppy doesn't sit … just walk away.

Try it again a few minutes later. If he doesn't sit this time, ask yourself, "does my puppy really know what sit means?" If not, remind yourself how young he is and continue to consistently use the word sit when he does it on his own … he'll get it.

Or, try luring the sit. Hold a treat (stinky is good, as it gets your puppy's attention) between your pointer finger and your thumb. Put that treat right in front of your puppy's nose. He will sniff it and try to take it. Hold on tight and lift the treat an inch or so straight up. Your puppy's nose will follow the treat, which will likely result in his butt hitting the floor.

Check out the video of a Lab puppy being lured into his first sit (and more) at **puppieschewshoes.blogspot.com** under "Links: teaching down/sit/stand". 🐾

Self-control? In a puppy?

Yes, it really is possible. The very best way for puppies to learn self-control is by playing with healthy, happy, well-mannered adult dogs. When interacting with an adult dog, a puppy who plays appropriately will find that play time continues. If the puppy bites too hard or plays too rough, the adult dog will warn the puppy to knock it off. If the warning doesn't work, the adult dog will end the play. If you don't have an adult dog to help train your puppy, here are some ways to teach your puppy to play nice (exhibit self-control).

Teach your puppy that good things happen when he sits.
What if, when your puppy runs to you, instead of jumping on you when he gets there ... he sits. Trainers talk all the time about teaching dogs incompatible behaviors. That means, using jumping on people as an example, a sitting puppy isn't going to jump on anyone. He can't. Jumping and sitting are incompatible. So, the next time your puppy runs toward you, grab a piece of dry dog food from your pocket or treat pouch and get ready. He's looking at you as he trots toward you and he'll see that you just did something with your hands that may involve food for him. Already you're changing his perception of what will happen next. Before he gets to you, take one step toward him. Bend forward as he gets to you, putting the treat in front of his nose as he comes to a screeching halt. Get that sit, reward it and walk away telling him he's a good boy. Teaching that basic behavior – sit when you get to a person – is the beginning of your puppy learning self-control.

Pushy puppies. Some puppies want to be in charge. Making sure that a pushy puppy has to work for everything he gets is a great way to create an atmosphere where you, the human in the house is in charge. That is, unless you want the four-legged who's only been on the planet a few months to be in charge.

What might a pushy puppy look like? How about a puppy who barks or jumps on you to get your attention? What about a puppy who brings a tennis ball to you and drops it at your feet waiting for you to throw it? And the one who nudges your hand to be petted? All of these things – while not so bad (and maybe even cute) when your puppy is little – will drive you crazy as he gets older ... and bigger.

Puppies do what works, so if jumping on you gets your attention, your puppy will keep right on doing it. If pestering you with a tennis ball eventually gets you to throw it, he'll keep doing it. What if you teach your puppy manners from go?

Start with teaching your puppy to sit before he gets any kind of food, treat or toy. Have him sit and wait before he goes outside and before he exits his crate. Training opportunities abound. Take advantage of your puppy's youthful enthusiasm and get those good puppy behaviors each and every day.

When your puppy can sit for several minutes, self-control is beginning to happen. Most puppies have no idea they can be awake and be still at the same time. We have to teach them it's an option. One of the best times to teach a puppy to be patient – to have self-control – is at feeding time.

Hand feeding your puppy, a few pieces of dry food at a time, not only teaches self-control, it:

- Builds the bond between you and your puppy
- Encourages your puppy to sit or down or both
- Provides a great opportunity to work on eye contact (say your puppy's name and he'll likely look right at you)

To see what hand-feeding looks like when you first begin, check out the video at **puppieschewshoes.blogspot.com** under "Links: Hand feeding".

Continued on page 36

ZERO TO 8 MINUTES AT BREAKFAST

Puppy: Callie
Breed: Lab
Age: 6 months
Scenario: Three-week board and train

Callie had very little self-control – pretty standard in pups. Fortunately, she was food driven. And after a good night's sleep, she was hungry. Perfect time to train.

Callie had a terrific sit/stay but a sloppy down/stay. This first morning of "board and train" she earned her entire breakfast as we worked on her down/stay.

Since tracking training results is extremely important, I pulled out the stopwatch. I put Callie's dog food in her dish but made it inaccessible to her. She could see and smell it but couldn't get to it. Next, I needed a baseline. I learned she could not down/stay for 30 seconds, so I backed it up to 20 seconds. It took many false starts until she understood that a piece or two of dog food would be delivered by me, by hand, only when she maintained the down/stay. Initially she popped up into a sit as I approached with kibble in hand. Each time she did, I put her back in the down/stay and started over. Finally, we got our 20 seconds. Then we got 2 minutes. Then 3 minutes 43 seconds. And the last down/stay that first morning, from which I released her for a potty break: 8 minutes 13 seconds.

While the above scenario played out, my two adult Labs were in down/stays about six feet from Callie. As we worked on the stay, I walked around the living room and eventually out of sight into the kitchen. Other dogs and my movement were intentional distractions. More distractions would be added as Callie got better and better at her down/stay.

One last word on self-control: When your puppy *offers* a good behavior without being asked for it – especially something that shows restraint or calmness – he is learning self-control. Example: You are at a park walking your puppy on leash. A mounted policeman is moving toward you. Rather than lunge on the leash or bark at the horse, your puppy sits and watches horse and rider go by. *That* is self-control. Reward these fabulous moments of great puppy behavior! 🐾

Those elusive house manners

So, let's say you have had dogs all your life. Did you train them? A little? A lot? Not so much? Or maybe there were dogs in your home growing up but you've never had one of your own. Or maybe you've never been around dogs at all. Whichever one of these applies, training this

particular puppy is going to be a challenge. Life with your dog – long term – will be far easier if you start your puppy off with basic house manners. Here are some of my favorites. I hope you will teach and reinforce these kinds of things throughout your puppy's first year.

Leash in the house. Whether you hold your puppy's leash in your hand or tether him to you (loop of leash on your belt and with the other end attached to his collar), keeping puppy with you in the very beginning teaches him a lot:

- *Boundaries:* He doesn't get to go anywhere he pleases in your home, only where you take him.
- *Self-control:* You stop walking and attend to something – say in the kitchen – he stays put. He can stand or sit or lay down but he can't leave. He may fuss about this a bit in the beginning but if you go about your business, totally ignoring him, he'll soon get it.
- *Leash 101:* He'll learn that if he doesn't want to get stepped on, he shouldn't walk in front of you – in that side-to-side fashion puppies seem to love. Better to teach this in the house than on a paved surface where, if he trips you, the road rash could be really bad.
- *Jump control:* When you stop moving, does your puppy jump on you? Drop the leash and stand on it. Stand on it so it's short enough that he can't jump but long enough for him to stand. Now comes the tough part. Ignore him. Don't make eye contact. Wait for a few seconds and you should become aware of a puppy who is no longer bouncing on the other end of the leash. You can also use this when you're seated – say at your computer – and your puppy jumps on you. Pushing him away won't work – he'll think it's a game. Your foot on the leash will work.

Move your butt. Teach this one early. It will make living with your dog way easier. Here's how it works at my house (the land of the big dogs). Let's say I'm rolling a suitcase through the house and there is a dog laying on the floor between me and my destination. As I roll toward the dog, I say "move". He does and I'm off to my bedroom to unpack. Fortunately, this is easy to teach.

Here's how to start. Let's say your puppy is off leash. You're in the kitchen and he is between you and a cupboard. Walk into his space, gradually skooch him out of the way using the word "move" as you make it happen. Do this anywhere and everywhere you find that he is in your way. You may initially be doing a bit of a dance with him but do this consistently and soon he'll understand that move means he should relocate.

TIP

When training a puppy to down or sit, deliver food rewards low, at nose height (hand moving toward puppy's nose parallel to the floor, not from above), to discourage the natural "pop up" or jump that often occurs.

Meet Stella. She a beagle mix whose mama was found on the streets. Mama and puppies were rescued and Stella is training to be a service dog. In this photo, she was four months old, staying with me for a couple of days of board and train. This was her learning to down/stay on a mat in my kitchen. Read more at **browndogtales. blogspot.com.** *Keyword: Stella*

Stay put. This is the opposite of "move your butt" and equally useful. Why? Because there is nothing worse than being in mid-stride over a 70-pound dog when he decides to stand up. Let's say you're walking toward your bedroom with a full laundry basket. Your dog is laying in the doorway. If he stays where he is, you can easily walk over him. Make sure that happens by including it when you teach down/stay. Get him comfortable with people walking over him. Practice this with all the members of your family. Once he understands that you're not going to step ON him, a quick reminder to stay should be all he needs when you approach with that laundry basket.

Never ask your dog to do anything you haven't trained him to do. In this case, your dog must have a solid down/stay before you teach him to stay put.

Kitchen etiquette. I've yet to meet a dog who doesn't like to hang around the kitchen when people are in it. It's such a good, smelly place and occasionally food ends up on the floor – something that will make most dogs smile and dive for even the tiniest morsel. The problem is, the kitchen can be a dangerous place for your dog. Let's say something boils over on a front burner and your dog is laying in front of the stove. Or you open the oven door to check on the turkey and he has his head in there before you can stop him. Or you're carrying the turkey from oven to counter and you drop it on his head because he tripped you as he was trying to sniff it.

Decide how to keep your puppy safe when you're in the kitchen. He can hang out with a family member in another room or you can:
- Teach him to down/stay in a particular place that is out of harms way but where he can still watch the action.
- Use baby gates to keep him completely outside the danger zone.
- Pop him into his crate with a stuffed Kong until you finish in the kitchen.

Meal time. Teach your puppy where he should be when you eat. It's perfectly acceptable for him to lay under the table or at your feet. It's not okay for him to beg or pester you or anyone else while they are eating. Whether you have dinner at the dining room table or in your favorite chair in the den, choose a place for your dog to be that doesn't encourage his dog face in your dinner plate. For example, you can teach your dog to down/stay on a dog bed or a mat (bathroom mats work well) next to your favorite chair. This can be especially helpful when the Chinese carry-out is on the coffee table – at dog-nose height.

Wait to be safe. Teach your puppy to wait for permission to go through doors. Why not just let him go out back to relieve himself? What's the harm in opening the door and letting him barrel past you?

First, teaching your puppy to wait at all doors will also discourage him from even thinking about bounding out of the car in places like your vet's parking lot, which is likely near a busy street. That's because you will have taught him that car doors are just like back doors: no going through them without permission.

And then there's this. You have company that includes your grandmother. Granny decides to let your dog outside. He bumps her as he runs past. She falls and breaks a hip. Keep granny healthy. Teach wait.

Puppies with self-control have learned that good behavior is rewarding. Here are training tips for just a few of the things that will help your puppy excel at being a well-mannered member of the family.

Leave it. Leave it teaches your puppy to look away or back away from something (with the implied and so important "don't put your mouth on it"). That "something" can be another dog, a cat, child, toy, food, anything and everything. Puppies are "nosey". If allowed to follow his nose without guidance from you, your puppy *will* get into trouble. Do you really want him to pick up the prescription pills you just dropped on the floor? How about your new cell phone or that nasty dead frog on the sidewalk? No. You want him to learn to "leave it".

Teaching it. There are many ways to teach your puppy to leave it. This is one. Put puppy on leash. Have a really tasty treat in your hand. Let your puppy smell it but don't give it to him yet. With your other hand, show him a toy, then toss it well out of his reach. Be prepared for him to lunge toward the tossed toy. Be a tree. Let him get to the end of the leash but no further. Say nothing. Don't pull him back to you. After a few seconds, when he turns to face you or comes back to you on his own, give him that tasty treat. If he continues to pull, say his name in a happy voice. When he turns back to you, give him a treat. Practice this often, adding the words "leave it" to the action.

Watch me. Watch me is eye contact between puppy and you. It teaches your puppy to look to you for guidance. If your puppy looks at you and you ignore him, he'll stop doing it, so keep your eyes on your puppy!

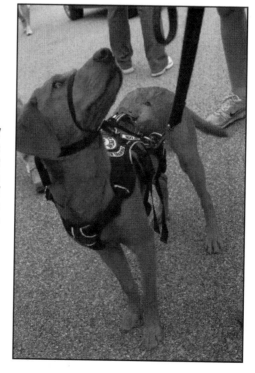

This seven-month-old Lab demonstrates a perfect "watch me" at an outdoor event with hundreds of people and a lot of noise – huge distractions for any young dog

Teaching it. Start with the name game. When your puppy is looking away from you, say his name. If he turns and looks in your eyes, reward and praise. Repeat, this time saying your puppy's name, then "watch me". When eye contact is made, treat and praise. Increase the time your puppy looks at you by withholding the treat for a few seconds. Practice every time you want your puppy's attention.

I've touched on just a few of the things you can teach your puppy to do. Training books, obedience classes, YouTube videos and dog trainers abound. Continue training your puppy in whatever way works best for you. 🐾

WARNING: Too much, too soon.

"MY PUPPY WON'T LISTEN to a thing I say when we're in the pet store. He has a great 'sit' at home. What's going on?" Sensory overload is going on. What exactly does that mean?

First, it smells. A pet stores smells like the ingredients in dog, cat and all the other critter foods. It smells like dog pee and dog poop and all the dogs from whom the pee and poop came. It smells like people and their clothing and what's in that baby's diaper over there. If the store sells fish, gerbils, birds, reptiles, etc., your puppy can smell all of them, what they eat and drink, as well as what they live in or on. If there is a veterinary office onsite, there are all those associated smells. And your puppy may smell fear, since too often some fool will show up with a dog who is scared to death of being in public.

It's noisy. It sounds like rolling things and voices, barks, growls, and whines. There is the sound of the automatic door opening, storewide announcements, stuff being shelved, dropped, and broken. There can be screaming children, talking birds, and all matter of noise pollution.

It looks weird. It's bright and crowded and there is stuff everywhere. And it's really BIG.

People behaving badly. There are people who think it's perfectly acceptable to rush your puppy, ooooh and awwww, squeal in a high pitched voice about how a-DOR-a-ble he is, try to pet him and maybe even pick him up, and possibly scare the living daylights out of him. If you are one of those, *knock it off.* When you meet someone in public with a dog, ask permission to pet the dog! If you see a dog in vest, read the vest and do what it says, i.e., "working dog DO NOT PET" or "ask to pet me."

Be a wise pet parent and introduce your puppy to his world slowly. For example, find a quiet spot – perhaps a neighborhood park on a week day. Keep your puppy on leash and invite him to sit or lie down near you. Check your text messages, make a phone call, or just relax and enjoy the moment. When your puppy settles, quietly praise him. 🐾

Training your puppy should be fun!

Do you want your puppy to come every time you call him? Develop his desire to enthusiastically come when called by playing games that make him WANT to come to you. Include the kids. They'll love it. Here's an example of a puppy training game.

Puppy ping-pong requires two or more people, one puppy and treats. Each person should have a few treats in pocket or hand. For very small puppies, their people can sit about 10 feet apart. For bigger or slightly older puppies, their people can stand. Plunk your puppy in the middle somewhere. If he trots over to investigate Person A, Person B should call puppy using the happiest of happy voices, clapping hands, and in general being silly. In the meantime, Person A looks away from the puppy, hands behind his back, completely ignoring him. This encourages the puppy to run to Person B, the fun, silly person. When he gets there, Person B should have a treat ready to give the puppy. As puppy finishes the treat, Person A calls puppy and the process repeats itself. Avoid puppy jumping up to get his treat by delivering it parallel to the ground at puppy-nose height, instead of from above – encouraging sit.

"Come" combined with sit on arrival – repeated consistently – will become puppy's default behavior for life. He will simply assume that when he runs up to a person, he's supposed to sit and wait for what's next. Rock on, puppy!

Lily

Tired dog, good dog

As the puppy encircling her water bowl illustrates, puppies sleep a lot. And when they wake up, they're ready to pee, possibly poop, and play ... whether you want to or not. My advice: go ahead and take the time to play with your puppy, wear her out, and she'll nap again. Then you can go back to what you were doing until she wakes again. 🐾

What's next? Things that – sometimes surprisingly – can scare your puppy and how to deal with them as they happen.

Ho ho ho, scary Christmas?

Maybe the big guy in the red suit IS scary to your puppy.

Think about it: big voice, beard, hat, funny looking clothes ...

Chapter 4

Beards and hats and statues, oh my!

Puppies freak out over the darnedest things ...

IT'S SATURDAY. The kids are hanging out with the puppy. All is well. Then the bearded brother-in-law comes 'round for a visit. He loves the kids and can't wait to meet the puppy. As he approaches, your puppy starts barking and backing up. You've never seen *this* before. You're apologetic. You're embarrassed. And you haven't a clue what's happening or why.

Your puppy's brain may well have been putting out a red alert: warning, warning, unknown scary looking thing approaching. Bark and back. Bark and back.

Puppies are visual creatures. They are constantly reading body language and absorbing their environment. Their response to what they see is a mix of the temperament they came with plus experiences to date combined with age and how the heck they are feeling (physically and emotionally). A puppy's response to something new can range from apathy to curiosity to anxiety to fear.

So what's the best plan to keep fear from happening? How can you prevent bearded brother-in-law debacles? Get that puppy out in the world. Introduce him to new sights, sounds, people, and places. Make sure every new experience is a positive one.

Your puppy needs to meet lots of people. Did you know that he doesn't view all humans as one big group that he either likes or dislikes? Puppies

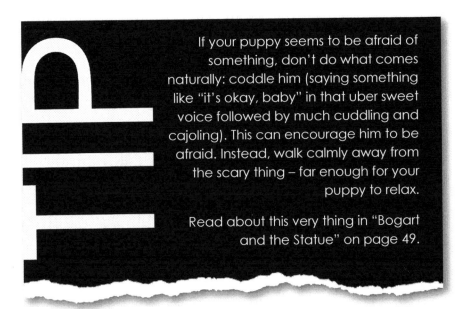

If your puppy seems to be afraid of something, don't do what comes naturally: coddle him (saying something like "it's okay, baby" in that uber sweet voice followed by much cuddling and cajoling). This can encourage him to be afraid. Instead, walk calmly away from the scary thing – far enough for your puppy to relax.

Read about this very thing in "Bogart and the Statue" on page 49.

consider age, ethnicity, gender and an individual's demeanor when they meet people. That means your puppy should meet a variety of:

- Babies, children, adolescents and teens
- Young, middle-aged and elderly adults
- Males and females
- Ethnically diverse people
- People in wheelchairs and using walkers
- People wearing hats, sunglasses, carrying bags, and pushing carts or pulling wheeled suitcases
- Men in beards and wearing hats (yes, fear can be this specific – a dog can be afraid of men with beards and afraid of nothing else)

Your puppy should walk on or in many different things, like:

- Concrete, gravel, sand
- Grass, dirt, mulch
- Mud puddles
- Wood, carpeted, and tiled floors
- Metal grates
- Wood, metal, and concrete steps both opened and closed

He should touch, mouth, sniff, and play with lots of things:

- Balls of a variety of sizes and textures
- Toys that make noise
- Cardboard boxes
- Empty plastic milk jugs and water bottles
- Hard rubber toys

Your puppy needs to go to lots of different places, including:

- Rooms in your own home that he normally doesn't visit (laundry room, basement, garage)
- The park, where he can see other dogs, people, and if there is a pond, maybe ducks and geese
- A ride on the interstate, so he understands the sounds of traffic, especially 18-wheelers and motorcycles

- Vet visits just to say hello. Ask everyone there to give your puppy a treat (when he sits politely, of course). You want your puppy to *love* going to the vet.
- Dog friendly businesses like sporting goods stores and home improvement stores

Your puppy should hear lots of different noises from a safe distance. At home you want your puppy to be comfortable with the sound of:

- The doorbell, vacuum cleaner, washing machine, garage door, and lawn mower

Out in the world, introduce your puppy to the sound of:

- Traffic
- A trash truck
- Construction site
- Trains and planes
- Sirens

Continued on page 50

When Aussie puppy Astro first saw this dog sculpture, he wouldn't go near it. After a few minutes of getting him comfortable around it, he moved in to check it out. See before and after videos on my YouTube channel. **www.youtube.com/dbogetti**

BOGART AND THE STATUE

Puppy: Bogart
Breed: Border Collie Mix
Age: 7 months
Scenario: first city training

Very Scary Stuff

Bogart's training up to this day had been primarily near his home in the suburbs. In the city for the first time, he was naturally curious as he got out of the van. But leash walking a puppy a new and noisy environment can be challenging. So we took our time, letting Bogart sniff and watch and listen.

Think about the kinds of things Bogart was experiencing for the very first time: smells (restaurants, truck exhaust, trash), sounds (honking horns, the clatter of trucks unloading), and sights (birds swooping in to feed on sidewalk leavings, people on bicycles, buses). Bogart took all of this and more in stride until he saw a statue on the sidewalk ahead of us.

He stopped dead in his tracks, staring, body stiff.

The first thing we did was back up a few feet putting some distance between Bogart and the statue. He sat, looking at it, sniffing the air. A minute or so later, Bogart rose and took a couple of steps toward the statue. We allowed him to absorb this new thing, approaching it at his pace, a few steps and sniffs at a time. As he and his mom made forward progress, I put a few treats at the base of the statue. In under ten minutes, Bogart walked confidently past the statue, then around it collecting his treats.

We spent an hour in the city that day and everything else went smoothly. In addition to overcoming the fear of something new, Bogart built his self-confidence that day and, as important, learned he could trust him mom.

Never, ever drag your puppy toward something that frightens him. Permanent fear issues can happen if you do.

Thinking to the future when your puppy is all grown up, discourage him from chasing or barking at stuff that moves, like:

- Kids on skateboards and bicycles
- Cars, trucks, motorcycles
- People jogging with or without a dog
- Sprinklers
- Kids playing soccer, baseball, basketball
- Squirrels, cats, etc.

Give your puppy the opportunity to be petted and held by lots of different people. Teach him that human touch is a happy thing. Be generous with belly rubs and massages. Make sure your puppy is comfortable being touched on all four paws, between his toes and inside his mouth.

Make sure puppy

- Gets to play with other puppies and well-tempered adult dogs
- Is left alone daily, in his crate, even it's only for a few minutes

Give your puppy the opportunity to climb, run and play – always in a safe and supervised environment. Let him play with a box – climbing in

"The frozen Kong stuffed with moist food and topped with peanut butter is like puppy crack. Worked like a charm" for Boogie the beagle.

and out of it. Make a cardboard box tunnel for him. When his legs are long enough, go up and down stairs with him. Play hide-and-seek with your puppy. Let him climb over obstacles, walk and later jump through a hula-hoop, crawl under a low table. Be creative. Have fun. He won't be a puppy for very long!

Avoiding separation anxiety. So far we've focused on things your puppy might fear. Anxiety can also have a negative impact on your puppy. One of the most common forms is separation anxiety.

Start your puppy off right by making your departures and arrivals no big deal. When leaving, simply crate your puppy and walk away. When you return, walk in without using that high-pitched, happy voice saying something like "Mommy missed you soooo much" ... while your puppy jumps, whirls and barks in his crate.

Instead, make your return the same as it would be without a dog in the house. Take off your coat, stash your briefcase, change clothes ... whatever. Return to the crate, wait for your puppy to settle before opening the crate door (this will become a "wait" at all doors), open the door and take your puppy out to go potty.

Crate your puppy for short periods when you're home to reinforce that the crate is a happy place and that you won't always leave him in it for hours at a time. Crate your puppy at night, preferably in or near your bedroom. You want to hear when he stirs in the middle of the night in need of a potty break.

Here are some other things to consider to keep your puppy's anxiety to a minimum:

- **Exercise** your puppy before crating him. A tired puppy will likely fall asleep straight away – avoiding anxiety upon your departure altogether.
- Although **TV** doesn't help all puppies, some are mesmerized by it. If your puppy watches TV, put his crate in a place he can watch it

while you're away.

- Some puppies prefer **music**. If yours does, leave the radio on. Or check out music specially selected and recorded to calm dogs of all ages at *Through a Dog's Ear.*
- Put a stuffed **Kong** in your puppy's crate with him.
- **Essential oils** can help a variety of anxiety and health issues. **www.experience-essential-oils.com/dog-anxiety.html**
- **Thundershirts** don't work for all pups but they work for many. Try one for any kind of anxiety your puppy develops. **www.thundershirt.com**

To better understand your puppy's body language and recognize anxiety when it happens, pick up *On talking terms with dogs: Calming signals* by Turid Rugaas. 🐾

And now, in Chapter 5, we turn to your puppy's wardrobe: collars, harnesses and leashes.

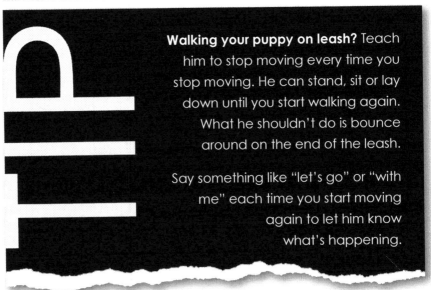

Walking your puppy on leash? Teach him to stop moving every time you stop moving. He can stand, sit or lay down until you start walking again. What he shouldn't do is bounce around on the end of the leash.

Say something like "let's go" or "with me" each time you start moving again to let him know what's happening.

THE AMAZING, INCREDIBLE KONG

Kongs are the best interactive toys ever. Get the Kong shaped like a snowman. Start with a red one that is appropriate for your puppy's size. The pink or blue ones made specifically for puppies will last a large-breed puppy about five minutes, so just start with a red one or a black one (for puppies who can destroy anything, anytime, anywhere). That's the definition of a heavy chewer.

Here is my favorite Kong-stuffing recipe: Pour a cup of dry dog food into a container. Cover it with steaming hot tap water. Put the lid on it and set it aside. When the food has absorbed all the water, it should be the consistency of turkey stuffing. Too wet? Add more dry food. Too dry? Add more water.

And now it's time to stuff. In the bottom of the Kong (where the little hole is), drop something really smelly and tasty like a dried liver treat. Your dog will be able to smell everything you put in the Kong so make it enticing.

Start stuffing the Kong tight with the moist dog food. Stop about mid-way and put something tasty in there like a drizzle of honey, a bit of tuna, or small pieces of apple. Fill the rest of Kong with moist food and cover the big hole up top with peanut butter or yogurt. Most important: freeze the Kong. This "pupsicle" is terrific for teething pups — the frozen Kong feels wonderful on their teeth and gums.

Stuffed Kongs are also good when company comes. A Kong can keep your puppy busy while you are visiting with your guests. A stuffed Kong can also help ease the anxiety of your leaving the house. Going out for a while? The very last thing you do is give your puppy a stuffed frozen Kong in his crate.

Does your puppy have diarrhea or constipation? Include plain canned pumpkin (NOT pumpkin pie mix) in his Kong.

Introduce puppy to lots of stuff.

Noise

❏ Trucks backing up
❏ Street cleaners
❏ Snow plows & snow blowers
❏ Garbage trucks
❏ Police cars, fire trucks & ambulances
❏ Motorcycles
❏ Sirens
❏ Fireworks
❏ Airport
❏ Loud speakers
❏ Construction site
❏ Train station
❏ Fork lift
❏ Lawn mower
❏ Power tools
❏ Gun fire

Get puppy paws on all kinds of surfaces

❏ Stairs: metal, wood, open & enclosed
❏ Sand, gravel, pavement
❏ Wood floors & decks or docks
❏ Tile floors
❏ Slippery/wet surfaces
❏ Manholes & grates
❏ Grass
❏ Mud & ice

Miscellaneous

❏ Car rides
❏ Boarding kennel
❏ Groomer
❏ Drive-thru banks
❏ Gas station
❏ Toll booth
❏ Outdoor restaurants
❏ Woods, fields
❏ Automatic doors
❏ Busy city streets
❏ Boat ride
❏ Playground
❏ Car wash
❏ Walk after dark
❏ A bridge
❏ The beach
❏ Hiking trails
❏ Sporting events

People

❏ Adults
❏ Babies
❏ Toddlers
❏ Children
❏ Teenagers
❏ Seniors
❏ Both genders
❏ Different ethnicities
❏ Police
❏ Firefighters
❏ Postal workers
❏ Vet clinic staff
❏ Crossing guards
❏ Meter readers

People with or wearing

❏ Umbrellas
❏ Sunglasses
❏ Hats
❏ Beards
❏ Costumes
❏ Shaved heads
❏ Raincoats/capes
❏ Canes
❏ Crutches
❏ Walkers
❏ Wheelchairs/scooters
❏ Service dogs
❏ Baby carriages
❏ Back packs
❏ Luggage
❏ Skate boards
❏ Shopping carts
❏ Bicycles

And anything else that your pup may experience in his life with you.

Lily

Chapter 5
Collars, Harnesses & Leashes

MOST FOLKS WITH PUPPIES are just twitching to take them for walks around the neighborhood. So how about we start at the beginning by ensuring that your puppy is comfortable in his collar? Ever see a dog who bobs and weaves when his owner tries to put his collar on? Why do you think that is and how might you prevent it?

Puppies can be hand shy (typically that means being uncomfortable when someone wants to pat them on the head). Does your puppy back up or duck when you reach for his head? If your puppy's natural instinct is to shy away from your hands, change how you approach him. Instead of bending over him and reaching for his head (a dominant posture to dogs), bend at the knees – getting more or less down to his level. Offer a piece of dry dog food or a treat in the palm of your hand, under his chin.

Scratch his ear or his butt while he takes the treat. Then do it again and again. All of this is nonthreatening and will help your puppy understand that human hands are good, not scary. This will help prevent a lifetime of your dog trying to avoid anything going on over his head.

One of the easiest ways to make that first collar-fitting easier is to sit with your puppy in your lap and treats at hand. Give him a treat and put the collar on with him facing away from you. The second the collar is in place, give him another treat. And another. The goal is that he associate anything that goes around his neck or over his head with good stuff. If you have a super wiggly puppy, this may be best done with two people ... one holding the puppy, the other offering treats and putting the collar on the puppy.

Now, what collars and leashes should you buy? Every puppy should have a **flat buckle collar** for everyday wear. Measure your puppy's neck to make sure you get the right size and check the fit regularly, since puppies grow fast. The safest flat collars are the breakaway variety, like the **KeepSafe**, shown here. Choking accidents can happen when two dogs are playing together or when a dog's collar gets caught on his crate, a fence, deck, vent, etc. Unlike other collars, the KeepSafe's buckle opens automatically if the collar gets hung up on something.

If your puppy is absolutely fabulous on leash, get him a **Martingale collar** for leash walking. When fitted properly, the Martingale is one of the best pieces of safety gear you'll ever buy. Why? Because your puppy *can't back out of it*. Don't leave a Martingale on your puppy when he is off leash. It will hang just loose enough for him to chew through it or get it caught on something.

The day that I saw a frightened German shepherd back out of her standard buckle collar in a pet store, run head-long for the front of the store and fly out through the automatic doors – straight into a busy parking lot – that was the day I started recommending martingale collars to my clients. Why was that German shepherd able to get out of her collar? Because her buckle collar wasn't tight enough to prevent it from slipping over her ears when she backed up, pulling hard on her leash. Something had frightened her that day in the store and she opted to run away from it.

That German shepherd would not have gotten away from her horrified owner if she had been wearing a properly fitted martingale collar. Martingales are comfortable for your puppy while keeping him secure on leash. They are made with two loops. Adjust the collar so the big loop will just slip over your puppy's head. Clip the leash to the O ring on the small loop and you're ready to go. If your dog tries to back out of his collar, the tension on the leash pulls the small loop taut, making the big loop smaller and tighter on the neck – preventing escape. When adjusted properly the dog is never choked, but the collar stays snug around the dog's neck (just behind the ears) until the dog stops pulling. The following illustration shows how the two loops on a martingale collar work, followed by a photo of the real thing.

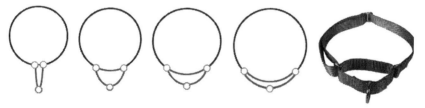

Want to see a seven-week-old puppy learning to wear a martingale and .... booties? Go to **youtu.be/JiEQKAH7wT4**.

If your puppy pulls when wearing a buckle or martingale collar, it's time to get working on leash skills. It also may be time to change the kind of collar you're using.

That's a Martingale collar above and head collar below. Head collars are not muzzles. On the next page is a pup wearing a front-fastening body harness.

Known as power steering for dogs, **head collars** – like the one modeled by the Lab puppy (bottom left) – can help you to have a puppy who never ever pulls on the leash. Wow, what a concept!

How is that possible? Head collars have two separate straps. One fits around the puppy's muzzle and the other goes around his neck. The leash is attached to a ring under the puppy's chin. A head collar won't choke your puppy because pressure is applied at the back of the neck, not to the throat. And the head collar is not a muzzle. When properly fitted your puppy can open his mouth to eat, drink, pant, fetch, bark, etc. The only thing he cannot do is pull on leash.

Head collars come with written and video instructions for proper use. Start using one wrong and it will never work. If you are unsure what "using it right" looks like, consult a trainer. Like all training collars, don't leave a head harness on your puppy when leash training is done. If you do, he will likely manage to eat it.

Should you decide you want a **body harness** for walking your puppy, choose a Halti, Sensation or similar model. The key to success with these harnesses is that the leash is attached to a ring on the chest. Why is that important? Because it's the dog's center of gravity. Uses? These harnesses are great for any pully dog, small people with big dogs, dogs with neck injuries and dogs for whom nothing else works. As with all gear, a body harness does not replace proper dog training. Learn more about body harnesses at **browndogtales. blogspot.com.** Keyword: harness

The other variety of body harness connects to the leash on the dog's back. These are perfect if you want to teach your dog to pull like a sled dog instead of walking politely.

When you've let your puppy get comfortable with his collar or harness around the house, teach him to sit and allow you to attach his leash to the collar.

There are many kinds of **leashes**. They come in every length

imaginable, in nylon, cotton, leather and all manner of natural and man-made materials, in every color of the rainbow and in patterns. They are thick and thin, wide and narrow, rolled and flat. Get what works for you. What works for me is a four-foot leather leash for pretty much any size dog. It's not too long, not too short and if not mistaken for a rawhide chew by a young dog, will last a lifetime. For folks with big, strong dogs, leather is kinder to the hands than nylon.

20-40 foot drag line. Drag lines, also known as training leads, are great for insuring that your puppy doesn't get away from you. They are meant to be attached to a dog's harness and allowed to drag behind him on the ground. You will never catch him if he decides to run away from you but you might be able to get your hands on that drag line.

Use a drag line in your own yard if it's not fenced. Taking your pup to the park where there is a big grassy area for him to play? Use a drag line there. Your dog has an extraordinary sense of smell. That nose can pick up the scent of a squirrel, a deer, a cat, a dog and steaks on a grill – all from a great distance. Keep him safe from his natural instincts which tell him to follow those smells to their source. If that's across a road, your pup can get hit by a car, since it seems all dogs are blissfully unaware that moving vehicles can kill them.

Warning: Never attach a long line to an inanimate object like a tree. Always attach it to a back-fastening harness, *never* to a dog's collar. Why? Because any kind of long line attached to a dog's collar can end in disaster. If he runs full speed toward something interesting (cat, bird, you, etc.) his forward motion can end badly. This happened the one and only time I bred two of my Labs – years ago. One of the puppies from that breeding went to live with a local veterinarian and his family. A few months later he called to tell me his wife had attached the pup to a zip line in the backyard. She went out to get the puppy a while later, only to find the pup at the end of that zip line dead, her neck broken. That beautiful puppy died because of human stupidity. Don't let the same thing happen to you.

Retractable leashes should be outlawed. Fortunately, their pros and cons have been written about a lot, so I'll send you to an article about them and you can decide for yourself whether you want to use one or not. Go to **puppieschewshoes.blogspot.com.** Puppy links: retractable leashes 🐾

Now that we've talked about gear, let's move on to the kinds of things to anticipate with almost any puppy. For starters they nip, bite and think little kids are their littermates. jmk

Chapter 6
Puppies nip and bite ... and other absolutes

PUPPIES ARE MOUTHY and puppy teeth are sharp. How are you supposed to survive unscathed until your puppy is finished teething, when the worst of the nipping subsides?

Start by having plenty of stuff for your puppy to put in his mouth instead of human body parts, table legs, remote controls, and the like. Redirect that puppy mouth to things like stuffed Kongs and treat balls. Some puppies love antlers (real ones, shed by deer, available at pet stores). Plush toys are okay with supervision ... but beware. Many puppies will shred them, pull out the squeaker and if you're not careful, ingest part of the toy. Also beware of stuffing pellets (very bad for puppy tummies).

If you buy your puppy tons of toys, will that stop his incessant nipping? Well, no. The more toys you buy, the more you'll see laying around looking forlorn because your puppy never plays with them. Why? Puppies have the attention span of a gnat. They're curious and when wide awake and fully rested, in constant motion. They're easily distracted by just about anything. Here's an example: your puppy is gnawing contentedly on his antler when he's buzzed by a fly that somehow got in the house. Boy howdy, that will get a puppy up and in motion in a heartbeat – often trying to catch that wily fly. So much for quiet time chewing his antler.

... *what fun is a tennis ball without a person tossing it?*

It's not unusual for a puppy to chew on or play with something for a minute or two and move on to something else. When that happens, how about this: play with your puppy. After all, what fun is a tennis ball without a person tossing it? If you have a fenced in yard and the weather is tolerable, go outside for playtime. That mantra – tired dog, good dog – applies here. Get him tired and he'll likely be ready for a nap instead of wanting to bite at your hands and arms.

Teach your puppy that nipping is unacceptable by stopping interaction with him the second you get nipped. No need to say anything. Just get up and walk away. You can also try screeching like a banshee when the nip lands (a really high-pitched "ouch" is good) and then ignore the puppy. Make it undeniably clear that calm puppy behavior gets attention from humans. Anything else gets nothing.

And then there's jumping

When your puppy jumps on you, he wants your attention, i.e., "hey, up there, look at me, down here, play with me!" Any kind of attention will do, even being pushed away. What to do? Immediately turn your back on the puppy and walk calmly away. When puppy approaches you again, before he jumps, ask for a sit. When he does it, tell him he's a brilliant puppy and give him a treat or his favorite toy or a belly rub – whatever he likes. Make sure all of this is low-key, since an excited voice may keep your puppy amped up and bouncing all over the place. Teach early and teach well that the appropriate alternative to jumping is sit and reward that sit in a big way. If puppy trots up to you, sits, looks at you, and gets no response, he will likely revert to jumping or some other unwanted behavior.

Consistency is the name of the game with puppies. *Everyone in the household must do the same thing or it won't work.* If one person rough-houses with your puppy – allowing and even encouraging jumping – your hard work to get rid of that behavior will be for nothing.

Kids and puppies

Kids tend to push puppies away with their hands. They also run away from puppies and squeal. To *your* puppy, these perfectly normal kid behaviors are an invitation for him to nip, chase and jump. So be sure to supervise all interactions between kids and puppies.

When your puppy plays with children matters, too. Your puppy will get up in the morning raring to go. He's well rested, has to pee, is hungry and wants to play. This is not a good time for your puppy to interact with little kids. He has way too much energy for that. Instead, have an adult take your puppy outside to run and play. Or take him for a brisk walk. A tired puppy is more likely to behave appropriately around children than a puppy with energy to burn.

Also teach your kids how to act around your puppy. If a child is too little to pick the puppy up, but wants to, suggest that he sit on the floor with the puppy in his lap. You don't want to end up with a broken puppy because an enthusiastic toddler dropped him.

Puppies have short attention spans and tire quickly. If yours has been playing nicely with the kids and suddenly turns into Evil Nipping Puppy, stop the play and let the puppy take a break. An over-tired puppy is pretty much the same as a cranky, tired two-year-old. Put your puppy in his crate for a nap. He may fuss for a few minutes, as he settles down. But if you ignore him, he should soon be sleeping soundly.

And then there's this. Since little kids have been known to shove a variety of objects into their own ears and noses, help them understand that things like Legos not only don't go up their noses, they don't go in any of the puppy's orifices either.

Diggers

Why do some puppies dig? Because they can. Or maybe they're bored or they want to get under the fence since everyone *knows* the grass is greener on the other side. Or because they are crittering (I smell a bunny, I do I do). Or it's really hot outside and freshly dug dirt is cool on a puppy belly. What to do?

- Don't leave your puppy alone outside for long periods of time. He will find ways to entertain himself and you won't like most of them.

- Make sure your puppy gets lots of exercise, both mental and physical. *Tired puppy, good puppy ... and one less likely to dig.*
- Stay with your puppy outside and focus on him – not your cell phone, the kids or the neighbor's dog. Instead, engage with him. Teach your puppy to play fetch and to play the "find" game. Your puppy can learn to find family members, toys, chewies – and pretty much anything else you want him to find. And when he's fetching or finding, he won't be digging.
- Interactive toys are terrific outdoors as well as indoors. Stuffed Kongs and treat balls are a great way for a puppy to entertain himself – unless he wants to bury them, which may mean providing him with a place to do just that.

You might want to consider creating a digging spot for your puppy. Pick a place in your yard appropriate for digging and put loose dirt or sand in that area (think kid's sandbox). To encourage digging in that spot *only*, bury some things your puppy really likes in the dirt (chewies, toys). Bury them deep enough that he'll have to work to find them. Walk your puppy to his new digging place and encourage him to dig. If he doesn't get it right away, show him what to do by digging with your hands where you know there is puppy treasure. Continue to encourage him to dig only in his special place. If your puppy digs near your favorite rose bush or tries to dig up your in-ground cable, consider a barrier of some kind in those areas to prevent digging.

If your puppy is obviously trying to practice his prey drive on moles and voles in your yard, do your best to get rid of those underground pests. Be careful that you use nothing that is toxic to your puppy when on your quest to de-mole and de-vole the yard.

If your puppy is digging a hole to lay in, perhaps he is spending too much time outside alone. Or he may simply be trying to stay cool. If that's the case, consider getting him a kiddy pool for cooling off. And always make sure he has plenty of fresh drinking water in a container that he can't tip over.

If your puppy is digging near a fence, he may – if left to his own devices – become an escape artist. Consider burying chicken wire underground at the bottom of your fence. Make sure there are no sharp edges that could cause your pup injury. Sometimes edging the bottom of a fence with big rocks prevents digging. Another option is to extend the bottom of the fence a foot or more below ground. But the very best deterrent for a digger is the presence of a person to teach him not to do it. 🐾

And now, on to driving safely with your puppy.

Chapter 7
Driving with your puppy

Here are five simple rules to keep your puppy safe when he rides with you. You may not like some of them but do you really want to take the chance of your pup dying because you screwed up?

1. NEVER EVER drive with your dog loose in the back of an open pickup truck. Ever. If you don't get why, you should be the proud parent of a goldfish ... not a dog. Oh, and if you're saying "hey, the dog's on his leash back there, attached to the side of the truck, so he's alright". Hmm, good going. Now instead of being thrown from the truck in a collision, he'll break his neck when you slam on the brakes.

2. NEVER EVER drive with your dog on your lap. And you say "But Fluffy loves to help me drive". Well then, since Fluffy is making the decisions ... has she thought this through? What

happens when you are in an accident and your air bag deploys? Fluffy will either be flattened or become a small, furry projectile.

3. Since you likely have a passenger-side airbag, put your dog in the back seat. Why? What happens when you are in an accident, your pup is riding next to you unrestrained and the passenger-side airbag deploys? There's a better than 50:50 chance of your dog being badly injured or killed.

4. NEVER EVER let your dog hang his head out a window because he likes to let his ears flap in the breeze. Why? Ever have a rock hit your windshield? I wonder what damage that rock could do to your dog's head? And then there's the possibility of him jumping out of the car while you're driving. Think that can't happen? Read "You can't make this stuff up ..." on the next page.

5. A TRAVEL HARNESS for your dog. Simple as that. The harness and the dog go in the back seat.

The great news for you and your dog is that in 2011 the Center for Pet Safety conducted a first ever Canine Automotive Restraint Crashworthiness Test. This is the only harness that passed with flying colors: the Sleepypod Clickit Sport. Learn more at **centerforpetsafety. org/research**

A good alternative to a safety harness is a crate. Small dogs can be crated in your back seat, as long as the crate is anchored to the vehicle so that it doesn't go tumbling when you take corners too fast or brake too hard. You don't want your dog hurling because he bounces around in there like he's on an insane thrill ride created for one purpose only: to make dogs miserable. Make sure he isn't sliding all over the place inside the crate by putting a non-skid rug (like a bath mat) in there for him to lay on. If your larger dog's crate will fit in the back of your SUV or van, that's a great option – again, as long as you anchor the crate.

Continued on page 72

You can't make this stuff up ...

The Brown Dog Blog. September 27, 2010.

I'm a dog trainer. When working with a new client, I stress the importance of keeping the dog safe from injury. There are more ways dogs can get themselves in trouble than you can possibly imagine. And I've heard way too many of them. This e-mail was in my box this morning. The client has an 11-month-old male Labrador Retriever.

> "We have to cancel our training for Wednesday. An unfortunate accident happened yesterday .... Bailey jumped out of the window of our car in the neighborhood and broke his femur. We don't know what he was thinking. He is going to have surgery today for his hip and neutering and will have a 6 week recovery."

Didn't know what he was THINKING? Seriously? He's a dog. He was thinking, "something smells really interesting over there and I'm gonna check it out" or "there's a dog ... I wonder if he wants to play" or a gazillion other possibilities. He had no clue jumping from a car could hurt him. He has people who are supposed to protect him from himself.

Do NOT let your dog hang body parts out of your car. Nor should you allow your dog to ride in the front seat. If you don't get that a dog distracting you while you are driving is not a great idea, think about this: a deployed airbag can seriously injure or kill your dog. Get your dog a harness that attaches to your seat belt system in the backseat of the car.

Why all the fuss about where your dog rides? Because there are enough ways for dogs to be injured without their people endangering them every time they get in a vehicle. *Of note:* if you are involved in a collision and your doors fly open, your dog will probably run from the vehicle. He will be frightened, possibly injured and definitely disoriented. He may wander off or be hit by another car. *Another scenario:* you are in a collision that renders you unconscious. When emergency medical personnel arrive, they are there to assist you, not your dog. If your dog is in his crate or tethered inside your vehicle, he stands a good chance of being cared for after humans are tended to. Make sure your cell phone includes an emergency contact who can take care of your dog in a situation like this. 🐾

Lily

Chapter 8
Food, chewies, first aid and more

There are so many different kinds of puppy foods, right? So where do you start? As I mentioned earlier, start by feeding your puppy the same food he's been eating. If you want to change his food after he's been in your home for a while, do it gradually. When you've identified a new food, buy the smallest quantity available. This is in case your puppy won't eat his new food or it doesn't sit well on his stomach. Start by feeding about a 60/40 combination of old and new foods. Spend a week or so increasing the quantity of new puppy food while decreasing the quantity of old puppy food. Keep an eye on your puppy's stools. They should be well formed, not soft.

How much should you feed your puppy? If you go with commercial food, start with the recommended amount on the bag or can and always measure. Then, pay attention to your puppy. He is unique in the way he burns calories, so he may need more or less than recommended.

Your puppy's nutritional needs will change throughout his first year. Puppies sometimes eat more during growth spurts than other times. If you find yourself saying, "He always seems hungry" consider that you may need to increase his daily food allowance, as he may be in one of those growth spurts.

After he loses his pudgy looking puppy shape, pay attention to his body build. With a few exceptions, most puppies should more or less look like their adult counterparts. Looking down on your puppy from above, there should be a distinct "dent" between the end of his rib cage and his butt and tail. That's his waist. If there's no dent, he may be overweight. If you can see ribs, he may be underweight. Check with your vet if you have questions about your puppy's weight.

Should you feed your puppy wet (canned) food? That's your choice. If, however, your puppy chokes on dry food, drinks excessive amounts of water or vomits after eating it – either wet down the dry food or switch to canned. The fastest way to wet down your puppy's dry food is, after you put it in his food bowl, cover it with steaming hot water just enough to moisten.

Why on earth would you want to soften your puppy's food? This is what I observed a couple of years ago with my senior dogs. They seemed to be drinking excessive amounts of water. That started me wondering about how efficiently they were digesting their food. I thought ... I wonder how much water it takes to soften dry dog food in a dog's belly? What if I added water to the food *for* them? I did it and their consumption of water dropped by a good 60% almost immediately. And no longer did my oldest dog choke on her food. Win-win.

If you are interested in feeding your puppy something other than commercial food, consult with your local holistic vet to ensure that your puppy gets everything he needs nutritionally.

If your puppy gets through his first year without diarrhea or vomiting, have a party. When he does have stomach issues, keep a close eye on him. Puppies dehydrate quickly. If he stops drinking water, get him to the vet immediately. If diarrhea persists for more than 24 hours, get him to the vet. At the first sign of diarrhea, switch your puppy from dog food to a bland diet. Canned bland dog food is available at your vet or you can make your own. To make your own, combine equal parts plain cooked white rice and cooked skinless, boneless chicken (boiled or microwaved). Chop the meat into wee little pieces, mix it with the rice (no seasoning, butter, etc.) Replace dog food with bland diet in equal parts. If you normally feed two cups of food a day, replace it with two cups of bland food. If your puppy has nothing more than an upset tummy (no nasty infections or blockages that require veterinary intervention), his poop should start looking normal within 24 hours of feeding a bland diet. If not, take him to the vet.

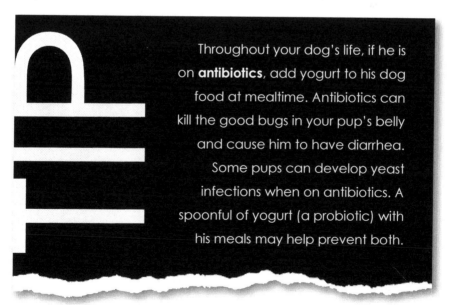

Throughout your dog's life, if he is on **antibiotics**, add yogurt to his dog food at mealtime. Antibiotics can kill the good bugs in your pup's belly and cause him to have diarrhea. Some pups can develop yeast infections when on antibiotics. A spoonful of yogurt (a probiotic) with his meals may help prevent both.

Chewies. A while back, one of my Labs nearly choked to death on a big slimy piece of rawhide. A while later he got a donut-shaped one caught on his lower jaw. After much twisting and turning, I finally got it off his jaw, swearing I'd never again buy rawhide chewies for my dogs. Fast forward a few years and I was happy I'd made that decision when it came to light that most rawhides for dogs are made somewhere other than the U.S. – often in China. The way they're processed in China is disgusting. Want details? Check out the article at **www.whole-dog-journal.com**. Keyword: rawhide

If you really want to give your puppy rawhide, try ones made by a company like Wholesome Hide. **www.wholesomehide.com.** The bottom line with rawhides: buy quality and *always* supervise your puppy because of the possibility of choking.

Antlers are a good natural chewie for your puppy, especially while he's teething. They're also good for most heavy chewers. Antlers are available at pet stores and online.

Want to give your puppy real bones? Before you do, learn which ones are safe for your pup. Check out integrative veterinarian Dr. Karen Becker's articles and videos at **healthypets.mercola.com**. Keywords: dog bones and chews

What else should you give your puppy to chew? Dehydrated sweet potatoes are healthy, as are whole raw carrots, and stuffed Kongs.

Understand that many things you give your puppy to chew might come with a choking hazard so one last time: supervise your puppy when he is chewing on anything. Don't leave bones or rawhides in your puppy's crate and leave him by himself. Instead, put a stuffed Kong in his crate if you have to leave him unsupervised.

Be an educated consumer. Dog food and dog treat recalls happen all the time. Don't you want to know if something you're giving *your* puppy is causing other puppies or dogs to get sick? Sign up for alerts from Dog Food Advisor. They'll send you a notice by e-mail when there is a recall.

If your puppy has **dry itchy skin, dandruff or a dull coat** it may be the food you feed. Or, it could be associated with a medication your puppy is taking or the time of year. When the heat goes on in your home for the winter, your pup's skin and coat may dry out. Try Grizzly Salmon Oil added to your dog's food daily for a shiny coat and healthy skin.

These are a few of my favorite things

There are a few things I've found that I wouldn't be without in my house full of dogs. You might find some of them useful, too.

If you have a dog, you should have a tin of **Bag Balm**. The stuff is magic for small wounds. Here's how I first learned of its effectiveness.

> Years ago, two of our female Labs had a bit of a disagreement. Teeth were involved and one of them ended up with a cut on her ear. That's when I learned how much a dog's ears bleed. The Lab with the cut on her ear started shaking her head and blood was flying everywhere. I ran into the house, grabbed the Bag Balm, ran back outside and slathered the cut with it. The bleeding stopped immediately and the Bag Balm (with a consistency denser than petroleum jelly) kept the wound clean. There was no need for a vet visit. The wound never got dirty or infected and it healed quickly.

EMT Gel or spray helps reduce pain and stop bleeding. Good for cuts and scratches, injured pads, hot spots, and even surgical incisions.

Benadryl for allergic reactions to bee stings, snakebites and swelling of unknown origin. Ask your vet for your pup's dosage, which is determined by his weight. Over the years, more than one of my dogs has been stung on the inside of the throat when swallowing a bee ... a good reason to discourage your puppy from catching and munching up on flying insects.

Vet wrap is a bandage that conforms to your dog's body and is used to wrap a dressing. It clings to itself, so keeping it in place is easy. This, along with Telfa nonstick pads for covering a wound, should be part of your first aid kit.

I highly recommend that you take a **pet first aid class**. I take a refresher class every few years through the Red Cross. There are also great pet first aid books for home and a Red Cross Pet First Aid app for your phone.

Moving on from first aid to the handiest house leash ever. Although you may not use the **slip lead** when your puppy is very young, you will find it handy at some point in his life. It's a leash and collar in one and fits any size dog. My dogs are fully mature and don't wear collars in the house. I keep one of these leashes by the back door and use it if I need to take a dog outside without looking for a regular collar.

Living with a doubled-coated breed of dog like Labs, I was forever buying a new brush or comb, always searching for an efficient grooming tool. And then came the **Furminator**. Check them out to see if they're right for your breed of dog.

Where should you get your puppy?

It took a while to figure out what should come last in my book about puppies. I finally decided I needed to talk just little about puppies from breeders vs. rescue puppies.

In recent years, I've had occasion to work with a lot of people and their purebred puppies. Sadly, too many of those puppies had some sort of health or behavior issue within their first year of life.

If you decide to go the breeder route, there is no guarantee a pup whose litter is registered – even one with an excellent pedigree – will be healthy of body and mind. Integrative veterinarian, Dr. Karen Becker, explains why a registered dog's "papers" are often meaningless.

> "Registration papers, whether from the AKC, the UKC or another registry, do not guarantee the health of a dog. This is a fact too many dog owners overlook. In today's world of puppy mills and online puppy storefronts, a 'papered' dog means nothing in terms of how the animal was bred, it's health, talents, or temperament."

Backyard breeders. This term outrages many people in the dog world. Here's my take. It depends on the definition.

Anything that remotely resembles a puppy mill – in the backyard, on the farm, wherever – should be eliminated from the planet immediately. Rescue the dogs, put the people out of business forever and press on.

And then there are the accidental pregnancies dogs experience (just like their human counterparts). These happen for a variety of reasons. Maybe nobody was paying attention to the female in heat. Or the owner believes in letting nature takes its course or doesn't believe at all in spay and neuter. Does lack of intent to breed two dogs mean anything at all? Only that there will be another litter of puppies that need homes. If that doesn't happen sometimes those puppies end up at a rescue or dumped on the side of the road. Sometimes they don't survive at all.

And then there's the guy around the corner who has a couple of dogs and wants to breed them. Just because they're good dogs. Here's where it gets interesting. Those breedings aren't always good. But sometimes they are. One of the best female Labs I ever had was bred in a situation like that. Maggie was smart, incredibly easy to train and had a work ethic that made her a kick-butt working retriever. And her temperament was such that she was as good hanging out in the house as she was hanging out in a duck blind.

So you just never know. Whether you're looking for a puppy from a breeder, a local rescue or your brother-in-law, use your common sense when picking that puppy. Don't have any common sense? Find a friend or family member who does and get their opinion before making a final decision.

How about puppies you might find at a rescue? I believe that your chances of having a wonderful adult dog in your life are pretty much the same whether you buy or adopt. The same goes for purebred vs. mixed breed. Some of the finest dogs I've ever worked with have been mixes.

No matter what kind of puppy you want, I beg of you: do NOT buy that puppy:

- **From a pet store.** Nearly all pet store puppies are from puppy mills. Buy a puppy from a pet store and the percentages go way up for major genetic issues both health-related and behavioral. You will also contribute to puppy mills staying in business. *Note: Adopting a puppy from a rescue at the pet store is totally different and encouraged!*
- **Online.** Online puppy stores are fast becoming the number one source of puppy mill puppies. Never, ever buy a puppy online.

To learn more about puppy mills (commercial breeders in it only for the money, keeping dogs and puppies in deplorable conditions), go to **browndogtales.blogspot.com**. Keyword: puppy mills

Dogs with jobs and dogs who compete. As your puppy matures and you find yourself with a bored dog, consider the kinds of things you can get involved in – together. Does your pup have tons of energy? Dog sports like agility are a great way to combine focus, play and exercise. Is your dog sweet and gentle and in love with all people? Consider becoming a therapy dog team. If your pup is a herding breed, there are competitions for that. What about teaching your Newfoundland to cart or your retriever to dock dive? Above all else, whether he's your hiking buddy or your lap dog, keep him close and love him. 🐾

And with that, new puppy parent, I wish you and yours a lifetime of joy
with your dog.

Astro

·

Index

V

Veterinarian 19
Vomiting 75

W

Wait 51
Wait To Be safe 40
Watch Me 41
Whole Dog Journal 76

Y

Yards 13

Dee Bogetti is a service dog trainer, consultant, and author. She lives with and loves three Labrador retrievers ranging in age from 9 to 13 years.

In addition to training people and their dogs and writing, in recent years Dee created an apprenticeship program for service dog trainers, a school access test with service dog health screening for service dogs, train-the-trainer workshops, and Brown Dog Tales, the newsletter.

Dee's service dog training book, *A guide to choosing and training your own service dog,* is available on Amazon.

Dee is a sought-after blogger, as well as a writer of poetry and creative nonfiction. When not training or writing, Dee enjoys woods walking with one or more of her dogs.

www.deethedogtrainer.com
puppieschewshoes.blogspot.com

Puppies chew shoes, don't they? is also available for Kindle.

A guide to choosing and training your own service dog
is available in print from Amazon.

Made in the USA
Middletown, DE
06 May 2017